SUCCESS IN LAW STUDIES

The 10 Keys to Top Grades

ELIMMA C EZEANI, Ph.D.

Lecturer in Law, Robert Gordon University, Aberdeen

DUNDEE UNIVERSITY PRESS
2013

Published in Great Britain in 2013 by
Dundee University Press
University of Dundee
Dundee DD1 4HN

www.dundee.ac.uk/dup

ISBN 978-1-84586-140-7

No natural forests were destroyed to make this product;
only farmed timber was used and replanted

British Library Cataloguing-in-Publication data
A catalogue for this book is available on request from the British Library.

Typeset by Waverley Typesetters, Warham
Printed by Bell & Bain Ltd, Glasgow

SUCCESS IN LAW STUDIES
The 10 Keys to Top Grades

Contents

Acknowledgements

I owe a lot to my teachers over the years, especially those who first answered my precocious question "What do I need to excel?" while I was studying for my undergraduate degree at Obafemi Awolowo University, Ife, Nigeria. In particular, I must mention one of the most dedicated teachers I have met, Dr Babafemi Akinrinade, who thoroughly explained how to answer the tricky law problem question. His explanation stayed with me all through my years of legal education.

For her patient review and unapologetic critique of this work, I thank my mum. As always, she ensured that I would keep to my long commitment to write this book. My thanks must also go to my colleague, Mrs Jacqueline Mackinnon, for her painstaking review: she made sure that my effort to condense a very broad range of material retained its focus. I am indebted to Dr Carole Dalgleish, Commissioning Editor at Dundee University Press, who saw the value in this work. This book would not have happened without her support and encouragement.

Finally, I must thank my father, who first made law so much more interesting than I could ever have imagined it would be. He was also my first teacher in so many invaluable lessons in life and in law, not least the importance of critical reasoning and logic. Daddy, this one is for you.

Introduction

This book has been an idea I have had for a long time; it is borne mainly out of experience, first as a law student and then as a law lecturer. Anyone who wants a law qualification wants to pass – and to pass creditably. Those institutions who offer law studies also want to turn out graduates who can compete favourably with their peers elsewhere, and those who teach law are mindful of their responsibility to assist towards this goal. This is the rationale for this book: that people who want success in their law studies can learn what is required of them in assessments. It may also be of help to the law teacher or assessor, especially for those early in their careers who may be not entirely certain of what to expect from a student and how to justify better grades awarded to one student and not to another.

There are many excellent works on how to learn the law. This one is about getting top grades. It therefore concerns itself not with techniques for studying the law but with those for passing law assessments, be they examinations, elements of coursework, quizzes, or even long-term pieces of research such as theses. Fortunately, law is as much a professional course in one country as in another and, wherever law is taught and assessed, the 10 keys explained in this book are relevant and of utmost importance. That is not to say that this book is a magic potion: a student's determination to excel; willingness to put in the hours of study required; and a keen interest to develop legal writing and presentation skills are all fundamental.

What this book does is to reveal what an assessor bears in mind when awarding top grades, some of which may be set out in a marking grid or model answer, but most of which are not because they may not be quantifiable. The law student who understands the importance of these keys and studies how they operate has acquired the secret of success in law studies.

1 Understand the Question

Lecturer: *"For class next week, read pages 303 to 450 and answer the questions that follow."*

Student ☹: "147 pages without pictures?"

For any student, and not just law students, the first and probably the surest key that will fit into the door marked "success" is to understand the question. In fact, once you understand what is being asked of you in any assessment, you are half way to passing and getting a good grade.

This is why you must never take the question for granted – the equivalent of charging down a dark tunnel at top speed without the caution of brakes: dangerous and usually fatal. Whether you are within the quiet walls of your room or in the tense atmosphere of an examination hall, take time to read the question and identify exactly what you are being asked. If you rush over this very fundamental first step, you will make costly mistakes. You may end up misinterpreting the facts, applying the wrong legal provisions, citing the wrong cases, or quoting irrelevant material. Take time to read the question and the instructions thoroughly. The following are pointers to help you do this:

RESPOND TO DIRECTIONS IN THE QUESTION

Note the approach you have been instructed to take in answering a question. An instruction to "discuss" an issue is different from one that asks you to "critically analyse" the same issue. You will certainly have to give a background and an overview of the essential details in both cases but a "discussion" requires that you address sufficiently the general elements of the issue while a critical analysis demands something different. For example, if you are asked to "discuss the implications of" a new piece of legislation, you are expected to consider it fully but broadly. On the other hand, a question that demands "analysis" requires an in-depth examination of an issue; it is usually specific in its focus. In Table 1.1, we can examine the common directives given in a law question and what they mainly require:

Table 1.1   Common directions and expectations

Question	Expectations
1. Discuss the implications of a new piece of legislation.	A general overview of the legislation is expected. Highlight the antecedents to the legislation; identify and examine its objectives. Consider the provisions and their impact. Assess the possible implications, including any adverse impact, the new piece of legislation will have for the relevant area of society.
2. Analyse the implications of a new piece of legislation.	Such analysis may include opinions that, for example, the legislation is not popular; that it will prove expensive to implement; that it will be a drain on available resources such as staffing etc. You may also point out, however, that the provisions are much easier to understand; that there is less likelihood of difficulties in interpretation by the courts; and that, despite its unpopularity, it is essential to society.
3. Critically analyse the implications of a new piece of legislation.	Students are often uncomfortable with the double-edged instruction to "critically analyse". Do not be put off by this: the only extra demand is that you will need to show that you are able to assess the merits and demerits of the issue in your analysis. So, while you have to analyse the said legislation from the perspective offered in Example 2 above, you should also highlight your findings based on the following assessments: How will the legislation work? What is needed to ensure that it fulfils the drafters' intention? Can it achieve its targeted objective? Is it enforceable? Is there a better alternative to the legislation as it stands? What problems can you identify with regard to implementation? Is it an improvement on previous legislation? If an amendment, does it address the targeted objectives?

4. Compare the implications of a new piece of legislation with a similar one in a jurisdiction of your choice.	Give a brief overview of both piece of legislation you have indentified for comparison. You will have to explain the similarities and differences between the two with regard to factors such as clarity, judicial interpretation, jurisdiction, enforceability, ease of implementation, remedies or sanctions, and so on.
5. Examine the implications of a new piece of legislation.	This is quite a wide brief, similar to that in Example 1. You have to include an in-depth evaluation of the legislation. Is it effective? On what grounds do you conclude that it is effective or not? Are there any real-life scenarios you can draw upon to assess the implications of the legislation, perhaps a recent event, a court case, a report in the media, academic opinion etc? Is the legislation going to change social behaviour? Does the way in which the legislation has been drafted make its implementation easier? Are its provisions susceptible to multiple or ambiguous interpretations? Are the courts going to find it easy to interpret and enforce them? Do you think the legislation is or is going to be effective in addressing its objectives?
6. Advise X on the implications of a new piece of legislation.	When you are specifically asked to render advice, you are first expected to address the legal principles and the issues raised in the question. A comprehensive examination of these is the foundation for the final piece of commentary you will make, ie the legal advice itself. However, note that you cannot give advice when you have not fully laid out the required considerations you have made, including the ones you have discarded. You may find that you will have to tailor your answer along the lines of the expectations in Example 5. The expectation is more or less the same when you are responding to a problem question with its specific detailed scenarios. We specifically address the problem question when we look at Key 5.

From Table 1.1, you can see that some of the answers may overlap. This is fine and is to be expected. Other directions may be given in a question: for example, "evaluate", "contrast" etc. A dictionary will easily tell you the exact meaning of any such words and you can, with the help of this table, direct yourself on the appropriate response to make.

Ensure that you are objective when you read the question. Do not put it in your own words or decide that you can rephrase the question better. Rephrasing may change the meaning and thereby affect your answer adversely. Also, do not be in a hurry to answer; make sure that you understand the question first. An extra 5 minutes spent over this will be so much more profitable to you. It will also do wonders for your grade.

FOLLOW INSTRUCTIONS

Part of understanding the question is also understanding the instructions and their importance. Pay attention to any instructions you have been given - you may lose marks for not doing so. Ensure that your word count is within the specified limits, and that your work is neatly presented in the format set out in your instructions.

2 Elements of a Good Answer

Lecturer: "So, why did you choose to study law?"
Student ☹: "I wasn't good at maths."*

A good law answer must exhibit as much clarity as possible, and as much formality as is practicable. It should leave the reader in no doubt that this is a law answer, not merely a general commentary. Below are some important points to note:

LEGAL PRINCIPLES AND ISSUES

As you read the question, try to pinpoint the exact aspect of law on which you have to focus. No matter how brilliantly you write, if you have not addressed the essential legal issues raised in the question, you will not score high marks. When you understand the legal principle that has been raised, you are more likely to understand the issues you have to discuss. As you read through the question, pause and ask yourself: "What does the assessor want me to do in order to be convinced that I know and fully understand the legal principle and issues arising in the question?"

For instance, take the following question in company law: "Discuss the role and duties of a director under the UK Companies Act." As we have seen from Table 1.1 earlier, the question leaves a wide margin for the student to offer his own opinion on the role of the director under the said Act. Yet, imagine an answer along the following lines:

> "A director is a director that is nominated under the UK Companies Act 2006. He is usually an important person nominated to do the work of a director. This is not a very good thing because a director will be answering only to the person who nominated him and so may not do a good job in his role. In my view, directors are usually concerned with their own objectives and don't always care about shareholders. Many of the corporate failures today are due to bad directors who have mismanaged the company when their role is to direct it ... "

---

* Not a very good answer here, especially as more and more law students may be required to understand the rudiments of arithmetic in certain law subjects.

The answer above does not indicate that the writer has a good understanding of the legal principles and issues arising from the question. For a good answer, the first thing to do is to identify those principles and issues by composing an answer along the following lines:

- Who is a director?
- What is the role of the director?
- Where is this role defined?
- Is this position defined in the UK Companies Act?
- Is there supporting interpretation or a definition of a director in UK case law?
- How have the courts interpreted this role?
- Are there any duties imposed by the law on directors when acting within their role as managers of the company?

Keeping within the precise scope of the elements offered above, we can demonstrate a better approach to highlighting legal principles and issues, as shown below:

> "According to s 250 of the UK Companies Act 2006 (hereafter referred to as 'the Act', a director includes anyone occupying this role in a company. This is a rather vague definition but it recognises the varied titles by which persons in a similar position of management in a company can be addressed. A director's role is to manage the company, which, as a juridical entity, is recognised by law, as the 'master' of the company. This was the view of the court in the case of *Dawson International Plc v Coats Paton Plc*, where the court held that, contrary to common opinion, the director is not answerable to the shareholders but to the company on whose behalf he acts. The articles of association of a company may set out specific duties for a company director, however, the Act has gone further in establishing statutory duties for directors under ss 171–177 ... "

Adopting the right approach by identifying relevant legal issues makes it clear that you understand what is being asked.

GOOD COMMAND OF LANGUAGE

Where you are studying for your law degree, or taking an advanced law course, you will find that formal language is preferred. The language of the law is objective, incisive and certain. Sometimes, there are references to other languages, most commonly Latin, to refer to some defined phrases. These may be italicised for emphasis but in any event must be written out correctly.

A good command of language is invaluable. Words are the tools of the legal trade: a word can significantly change a sentence. The student who can apply a variety of apposite words and phrases in answering a question stands to gain better grades. You cannot write a law paper in the same way as you speak. While it may be easier to explain things with jargon, when answering a law question you must avoid this. You need to ensure that you communicate your arguments as clearly as possible and so obscure words and phrases, and even mere colloquial, everyday language, are best avoided unless absolutely necessary. Such necessity may arise, for instance, where such a word or phrase is the subject of contention or is fundamental in answering a question. An example might be whether a word in ordinary usage could be interpreted as a racist remark. Nevertheless, you must choose your words carefully. If you find that your range of vocabulary is limited, a good general dictionary will help you to choose the best word to express yourself. Note, however, that you still need a good *law* dictionary to ensure that you are using legal terminology properly too, as we will reiterate later.

CLARITY OF EXPRESSION

Ensure that your sentences represent exactly what you need to say. For written work, in particular, do not write as though you are in conversation with your friends. A law paper full of "don'ts" and "can'ts" and other such abbreviated words is not attractive. Eliminate these from your written work. Also eliminate high-sounding phrases and idioms that you may think will make you the star at the bar (by this I mean your local drinking establishment and not the association of legal practitioners) but which only show that you know some big words. Avoid pompous language. This is a common pitfall for the law student – and it can make your work unintelligible. There is also a risk of having your ideas misinterpreted. It is better to be as simple as possible so that whoever reads your work can immediately understand your thoughts and the ideas you have put forward.

A good legal paper should never be obscure. If the assessor cannot understand what you mean, it will be difficult to score you highly. You must aim to be understood. Be as clear as you possibly can. It may help to say or to read your written words out loud before submission.

ORGANISATION AND COHERENCE OF IDEAS

Avoid long-winded sentences and over-repetition. The person marking your script wants to be impressed, not depressed. Avoid going round in circles – repeating a point over and over again. This makes your work unwieldy. The same will happen when you jump from one idea to another without establishing a link between ideas. Your paragraphs must also link, one with the next.

It will be difficult to succeed in legal studies without mastering the art of coherence. A common error is to present ideas as they occur to you and to leave it at that without editing. This does not make for a good piece of work. For instance, when writing a paper where you have a number of issues to discuss, one idea must evolve to the next. If you have to refer to a previous idea or thought, you must state that you are doing so. It is also good to explain briefly why and how that previous idea is relevant at the present time. Also, if you wish to introduce an issue which you intend to discuss at a future point, explain that you will elaborate more on that idea in due course. This way, all parts of your work form a unified piece and make sense to a reader or assessor.

THE BENEFIT OF A LAW DICTIONARY

As mentioned earlier, you will need a good law dictionary. There, you will find the appropriate phrases and terminology for your use. You will also find the appropriate legal meaning of words and expressions; some common expressions may not reflect the appropriate legal circumstances and, when misused, can ruin a good piece of work. For example, in contract law, "consideration" refers to what is given in order to obtain something. In a contract of sale, this may be the "price" of goods. However, if a student refers to "consideration" according to the ordinary meaning of the word, ie "thinking something over carefully", it is obvious that this does not reflect the intended meaning in contract law.

Where you use the wrong expression or refer to maxims in the wrong context, you will only lose marks. A good law dictionary is therefore essential.

REFERENCE TO GOOD LEGAL SOURCES

You need to understand how the law is written and how it is spoken. A good understanding of case law and how to read case reports is also fundamental. We will examine legal sources as authority more fully in Key 3. For now, get used to the ideas of reading good law textbooks, and of researching the cases you come across. Apart from being secondary sources of law, law publications are also important as they help you to appreciate the language of the law. It is in peer-reviewed journal articles and legal opinion that you will see how those who have mastered the language of the law make the best use of it. Academic publications help the student to understand the application of legal principles and demonstrate good legal writing. However, be warned – it takes a while to develop the skill of legal writing. Do not be in a hurry or attempt to copy the grammar you read. Legal writing skills will develop as you work.

Make good use of the library. Modern technology and the internet have made a huge number of materials available online. It is good practice to get a feel for how to write about law and even how to speak about the law by availing yourself of the best of these materials.

EDITING AND PROOFREADING

Even in on-the-spot assessments such as exams or class tests, leave some time for editing your work. Now, this is not just about reducing the work so as to fall in line with the stated word length, although, if the latter is given, you must comply with it. Editing and proofreading your work help to determine what is absolutely unnecessary – a lot of reference material may be good for background research and reading but do not necessarily have to make their way into your work. This is so especially where you have a good number of sources all saying the same thing – one or two of the most important ones will suffice.

Some students may be fascinated with reproducing case law and, indeed, you may find that your tutor may like to see a good number of cases referred to in your work. However, it will not always be necessary to reproduce more than two cases when discussing a single *ratio decidendi*. The opinion in academic writing should also be approached in the same way; if five people hold a similar view, it may not be necessary to reproduce all five. If writing a long essay such as for coursework, or even a thesis, you can refer to the main one in the body of the work and refer to the rest in your footnotes.

Finally, check and re-check for spelling, grammatical and typographical errors.

PRESENTATION

Aim to keep your writing elegant and attractive. It is good practice to use headings and sub-headings in your work. This enables you to concentrate on one issue before passing on to another. It also makes your work easier to read. This does not, of course, mean that you should set every three sentences under a sub-heading; that way, you will just end up with a ridiculous-looking piece of work. Use sub-headings judiciously. Italicise or underline cases and foreign phrases so as to distinguish them.

If your work is handwritten, ensure that it is legible. Avoid smudging your work, whether with your hands or with ink marks. To avoid the latter, an extra pen taken into examination halls can help. Use simple, easy-to-read fonts for printed or typewritten work and make sure that your work appears neat and tidy overall.

3 Legal Authority

Boy: "Let's buy the green curtain. It'll make the room cooler."
Law student girlfriend: "And what is your authority for that?"

In order to present a good piece of work, you will need to refer to appropriate legal authority. Legal authority, or what can simply be referred to as your sources of law, can be categorised into two types: primary and secondary sources. As is implied by the name, primary sources are the first and most important sources. They contain the law as it is and set out the applicable principles.

PRIMARY SOURCES

Primary sources are legislation and case law. Legislation, in particular current legislation, sets out the law; it is important that you refer to the legislation that is currently applicable at any given time. Always check to ensure that you are consulting the relevant piece of legislation; there may be several related laws on one topic and you need to identify and refer to the specific instrument you require. Case law is particularly important in common law jurisdictions, where judicial decisions have largely formed the law and continue to do so. They reveal how a particular point of law has been interpreted and applied in real scenarios.

SECONDARY SOURCES

A very good source for legal authority is the peer-reviewed journal article. This is because articles are often researched papers and can reflect past, present and even future positions on the law. A good article will also address its topic objectively, and reach a definite conclusion on an issue. This makes it a clear and unambiguous source for you. Of course, you must ensure that you read articles from credible sources. Too often, students are lured by search engines, web pages, and blogs that, on closer inspection, do not engage with a deep objective assessment of the law but merely offer private, unsubstantiated opinions. Avoid these. Most libraries now have online facilities that offer access to many electronic collections and databases, including law reports etc. Make use of these ones.

Textbooks and monographs are excellent sources of past and current developments in law. The textbook expounds on the law and discusses general legal issues more fully. A monograph is a more specific text which is focused on a single topic and will usually be informed by extensive research on the issues related to that topic. Note, however, that these are not, in themselves, the main sources of law. A common mistake is to refer to a legal provision and cite the source as a textbook written by a certain author. This is bad practice. The law is found in legislation – in the statute or rule or other legal instrument itself; it is the legal instrument that is the source of law not the textbook.

DISTINGUISHING BETWEEN OPINION AND FACT

This is a fundamental skill in legal studies but is especially relevant in studying the law of evidence, in particular the admissibility of hearsay evidence.

A very common occurrence in day-to-day life is the confusion between fact and opinion. Consider the following statement:

> "I have never been to India but I know that there are lots of cows there. I know this because my colleague, who is very intelligent, thinks so."

This simple statement is factually inaccurate. You cannot "know" for a fact that there are cows in India on the basis of the opinion of your colleague, regardless of how brilliant that colleague is. A truer statement would be:

> "I have never been to India but I am told that there are lots of cows there. My colleague who, is very intelligent, says so."

One thing to watch out for when consulting legal sources is an author's purely subjective opinion. You must be able to distinguish between what the law is and what a writer says it ought to be: these two are very different things. This is why referring to the primary sources is fundamental – if you know what the law says, then you can easily identify when a writer is merely giving an opinion on it. You can refer to that opinion in support of your arguments or to point out a contrary position – but do not present an opinion as fact.

4 The Law Essay

Question on the law of agency: "Who is an 'agent' in law?"
Answer: "An agent is a person who works for the government secret service."

Unless instructed otherwise, questions for law assessments are typically to be answered in essay form. An essay is a long piece of written work and will cover as much ground as the question expects. However, the essay is not simply a chance to write everything you know on a given topic. There are limits to what you can do and how far you can go in setting out your answer. Although it may appear (depending on how long the essay should be) that the essay question offers a wide scope, a good law essay has a clearly defined objective and will not lose its focus. It must also reflect a good understanding of the relevant legal rules and principles applicable to the topic on which you are writing.

The following three steps which apply to essay writing in general are a good guide to structuring your law essay:

INTRODUCTION

Your essay must be introduced properly, in order to help the reader know what you are going to talk about and how you have set out your answer. This means that, more often than not, this preliminary element in your essay may well be better constructed once you have reached the end of your piece of work! Once you have actually finished writing the essay, you can tell how you have set out your subsections, and how one issue connects with the other, and you can state clearly what your final conclusion is.

The introduction for an essay should not be too long – ideally, no longer than a paragraph, or two at most, unless you are writing an extended piece such as a thesis where the introduction can run into a few pages. Be clear on what you have done in the essay, and highlight the layout of your work. Longer essays such as research theses may have the introduction running into several pages but they must still reflect these rules: say what your focus is; identify the issues you tackle; and outline the steps you have followed in your work.

THE BODY OF THE WORK

It is always beneficial to give a brief piece of background to your essay – a quick insight into its basic foundations. Since it is not the main issue that you have to address, do not spend too much time on this: it really should not take up more than a few sentences. Go on to your main issue and be careful to maintain your focus. This is a law essay and the law requires facts and objectivity, not guesses or pure conjecture. While the aim is to produce an original piece of work, state the facts and the law as they are and not as you think they "could" be, or "should" be. (The higher you progress with your studies, the greater becomes the demand for originality. A Ph.D. thesis, for example, must form an original contribution to knowledge – a task which sounds daunting but which, with a lot of work, may be much easier to achieve than you may fear.) Exceptions may be made for closed-book examinations, where a student need not necessarily state verbatim (word for word) the provision of the law or the decision in a case. Even at that, you must be able to refer to the law in such a way that you leave little room for the marker to doubt whether you actually know what you are saying.

Remember that you must not merely reproduce what has already been written on a subject. In extreme cases, this may amount to plagiarism, where elements of other authors' work are lifted and reproduced without properly acknowledging the copied portions (see Key 10). You want to present a summation of all that you have read while doing your research for the essay and you need to be able to do this convincingly. You also have to ground your arguments on hard evidence. What does the law say on the issue? Have you analysed the facts accurately? Is your interpretation of the facts and the law logical? Always ensure that you do not stray off the tracks: stay focused on the key issues to be addressed.

CONCLUSION

Your conclusion allows you to round off your arguments. It is not a place where you introduce new material – this only makes for an illogical piece of work, since the previous content would have not made any reference to such new material in the conclusion. A good conclusion gives a brief recount of what has been said and then goes on to establish your final position as suggested or indicated in the prior parts of your essay. Where you are expected to establish a definite position, you need to come down clearly on one side of the argument or the other.

Even where there has been no clear-cut instruction on how you are to end your work, it is still important that your conclusion is a logical end to your preceding arguments. Check that anyone reading your work will be satisfied that, at this point, you have done what you set out to do. Your conclusion must show that you have actually answered the question.

5 Problem Questions

Question: "Consider the following scenario. Advise the parties."

Answer: "This is a serious case. I advise the parties, in their own interests, to find themselves a very good lawyer."

You may think that the problem question is a landmine. It is not. The problem question only sets out a scenario and asks the student to render advice based on knowledge of the law and a good assessment of the facts presented. When faced with a problem question, the first thing to do is to determine the specific area of law to which the question relates. Then, pay attention to the salient parts of the scene set out: not everything that happens in the scenario will be directly relevant. Some circumstances or events in the question may not have much to do with the legal issues you have to discuss, although they help to set out the scene. Ignore these.

You will probably be asked to "advise X" or "advise the parties". We mentioned this in Table 1.1 in Key 1. In a problem question, the objective is for you to determine what advice is best suited to the circumstances but only *after* you have fully assessed the issues that arise for determination; considered the applicable legal authority; and applied these to the scenario before you. Admittedly, this leaves you with little room to manoeuvre because if you cannot immediately identify the area of law relating to the given scenario and therefore cannot pinpoint what rules apply, you will be in some difficulty. However, do not be put off by a problem question when you see it. If you understand how to approach it, the problem question can be very straightforward.

Use the details of the question – refer to the parties by the names used in the question. Using the information given in the question shows that you have engaged with the circumstances. It also makes it easier for you to get a feeling for the scenario as though it were real.

To help you with approaching the problem question, think of your task along the lines of responding to what can be referred to as the **IRAL** rule: **I**ssues; **R**ules; **A**pplication; and **L**egal Advice. You may come across other guides and approaches to answering the problem question, including a more common variant of the one discussed here – **IRAC: Issues; Rules; Application; Conclusion.** I prefer to refer to the last segment as "Legal Advice", not "Conclusion", since you are expected to provide advice at the end of your answer and not merely to bring your considerations to a close

ISSUES

It is important that you note down *all* the legal issues raised in a question. First, this means that you can follow a clear road map when you are discussing the issues subsequently. It also lets the person marking your script know that you do have an idea of the relevant issues in the question. For a contract question, for instance, the issues may involve validity of contract; whether an offer has been made; whether consideration has been given; or whether the contract is void or voidable. Write down the relevant issues at the start of your work. As mentioned earlier, bear in mind that "issues" must not be confused with the mere details in the question. For example, consider the following excerpt from a question:

> "Jason is a married company director of Inc UK Ltd and loves flashy red cars. His company car is a blue Porsche with 16-inch alloy wheels, twin turbo engines and a front-loader injector system which is the newest technological advancement in front-wheel engineering. While driving to work on Monday morning, he was chatting with his mistress on his iPad when he lost control of the car and crashed into a cyclist. The Porsche lost its front bumper. The cyclist has sued Jason and Inc UK Ltd, jointly and severally, for the injuries sustained to his legs."

It is easy to become distracted with the extensive descriptions of the company car and Jason's morals (or lack thereof). The question is essentially on the scope and extent of vicarious liability under UK company law and a good answer should therefore focus its discussions around this issue.

RULES

State the relevant authority relating to the issues you have identified. As previously mentioned, your authority should be derived, first and foremost, from primary sources of law, ie statutes and case law. In the excerpt above, the UK Companies Act 2006 is the main legislation on company matters. There have been a number of cases on a company's vicarious liability under UK law and the smart student will note and discuss the definitive opinions of the courts in such cases.

APPLICATION

This bit of your road map is crucial. Most students make the mistake of answering questions in isolation, ie without making direct references to the scenario they are considering. In our question above, Jason is a company director of Inc UK Ltd. These points should be clearly referenced in your answer. Do not talk about "a director", or "a company" when you have been told the names of these parties. It may be necessary to point out that Jason was driving not just "a car" but the company's blue Porsche. (The specifications of the car may be relevant if there was a dispute as to the particular make or model of the car, ie if these were in issue. Since the question has not suggested such a dispute, do not raise it.) Apply the rules you have identified to the particular circumstances of the problem question. You do this by drawing comparisons or distinctions between relevant case law and statutory provisions and the circumstances of the question. For instance, when considering whether Inc UK Ltd bears any liability for Jason's accident, you have to consider the circumstances under which a company can be held legally responsible for the actions of its employees. This will arise under the doctrine of vicarious liability, an aspect of the law of agency and of the law of tort or delict. Do not be tempted to cite all the cases on vicarious liability. Some markers do find this impressive and the main cases to which your tutor is partial may be of assistance! However, be conscious of how much time you have available to you. An extensive analysis of one issue where there are three others left untouched will not earn you full marks. There are limits to a marker's sympathy.

LEGAL ADVICE

This is where you reflect on all you have considered earlier and present your summation of the facts and your final advice. In the problem presented above, a good conclusion would be along the following lines:

"On the basis of the authorities above, therefore, it appears that the cyclist has a good basis for an action against Jason and Inc UK Ltd. By relying on the authorities cited above, the cyclist can claim damages for ..."

Referring to your earlier analysis of the scenario helps to make your final advice stronger and more convincing. Note that you do not need to set out your answer using the above four pointers as sub-headings. They are just to guide you on what you should address in a problem question.

6 Legal Content

Student's query: "Just tell us exactly what a good law paper must have!"
Tutor: "That's easy. Legal content."

While you are may not be expected to know all of the law on a given subject, you must be able to find the answer to the question you are asked and to present it properly: so you have to know how to *apply* the law. It is also not enough to be able to cite cases: you must understand the material facts, the *ratio decidendi* and any relevant *obiter* statements, and be sure of the final decision reached in the case. In short, your answer must be a clear demonstration of legal analysis. There are three important factors that can help here: up-to-date knowledge of the law; objective review of existing literature; and critical reasoning.

UP-TO-DATE KNOWLEDGE OF THE LAW

One of the first things you will encounter in law studies is that there are general rules but there are also exceptions to each general rule. You will notice this when you read though some legislation and find the subsections or sub-articles which provide for exceptions to the main position of the law on an issue which is typically set out in the main section or article. With case law too, you may find that the courts will, at times, depart from a previous position or suggest an alternative to a previous interpretation of the law. This is why it is vital that you know the current position of the law on a subject – both the general rule and any exceptions or amendments. Check to see whether there have been any amendments to relevant legislation and cite the appropriate provision. Where a decision on a point of law has been amended or a judgment overturned, you must be able to state the new position. Always ensure that the authority you cite reflects the present legal views on an issue. This is why law relies more heavily on primary sources – because in legislation and case law the relevant position of the law is clearly stated.

Legislation and other subsidiary material, case law and commentary, legal opinion from academics, or exposition and evaluation of legal issues, are the basis of a critical law essay. It is very easy to offer up one's views or to repeat commonly held opinions but these do not suffice for a good piece of work in law. An assessment paper must reflect sufficient legal content. This point is important especially given the increase in cross-disciplinary studies such as Finance and Law, Management and Law etc, where students will have to pass both the legal and the non-legal elements of the course. Where you are being assessed on the legal aspects of your course, the issues you raise and discuss must reflect an awareness and understanding of relevant legal material on the subject.

OBJECTIVE REVIEW OF AVAILABLE INFORMATION

Every answer to a question in law studies must exhibit this important element: objectivity. Test the information you have gathered while doing research for your work. Ask yourself the following questions. Is this article expanding on, or providing a counter-argument to, the main issue here? Does this academic writer throw any new light on the topic? Has this case suggested an alternative position, even if that alternative was not applied? How has this piece of legislation changed the legal landscape? Has this principle ever been applied or has it proved to be impracticable? Can I find support for my position? Is my view the common view? What is the possible argument on the other side?

It is very easy to be subjective when you are faced with a sensitive issue, as some law questions can turn out to contain. It is important to hold back on your first impressions or opinion when approaching a law question, to ensure that you have given full consideration to the question before you. One of the most common errors in legal writing is to give full rein to your emotions or to rely on whatever is the common opinion on a topic. Often, students will provide arguments which are really their own subjective perception on an issue, or the perceptions of their friends, family or the public. They are disappointed when they do not score as highly as they had hoped for what appears to them to be a very obvious point.

Take, for instance, the following question on human rights:

> "The Government of a country is responsible for protecting its citizens. Examine the Universal Declaration on Human Rights (UDHR). How has the UK [or your country] applied the provisions of the Declaration in its domestic regulations?"

A student's answer may immediately, without providing the basic framework for the answer set out above, launch into an attack on, or praise for, as the case may be, the UK Government's protection of human rights. It may give several examples of racist behaviour and mention a number of cases that have been publicly criticised for being too lenient in upholding the human rights of convicted persons over their victims, for instance. These pieces of information may all be available on the web, on the radio, or even, as mentioned earlier, public opinion. However, they will not suffice for a good law answer; the discussion must be substantiated by law.

A good answer must first identify the non-binding nature of the Universal Declaration. This means that while the provisions have been agreed by the United Nations Member States, the provisions are normative and exhortatory; they are not legally binding. A country may therefore recognise the provisions of the UDHR but not include them as legally binding provisions within its domestic law. However, where the provisions have been incorporated in some form into the legal system of a country, the provisions of the UDHR then assume greater domestic significance. In the UK, for instance, the European Convention on Human Rights (ECHR) incorporates elements of the UDHR. The UK has introduced the provisions of the ECHR into the UK domestic legal framework through the Human Rights Act 1998. In essence, however, the UK is not bound by the provisions of the UDHR but is bound to comply with the provisions of its own domestic human rights legislation.

An objective review is achieved where you have considered both sides of the argument on an issue, always within the background of supporting legal authority. The following reflections are an invaluable aid: What is the position of the law on the issue? How have the courts interpreted this position? Has a commonly held view on an issue been criticised? What are the contrasting views on a particular subject?

If you have attempted an objective assessment, you are better placed to make a credible conclusion on a question.

UNDERSTANDING AND DISTINGUISHING CASES

One of the crucial skills that make for success in law is to be able to distinguish cases. To do this, however, you have to understand the principles behind a case and know how to read case reports. A case may appear very similar to the facts of a problem question you have but it may not be so: judges sometimes agree on a principle of law but then apply the principle differently, depending on the merits of a case. Note also that cases that have been listed for further reading, for instance on lecture slides or in handbooks, may not necessarily be in support of the principle you have been studying – they could be against it. The tutor may have included them to provide a counter-argument or to show where a court has departed from the common position; you will only be able to know this if you actually read through the case reports!

Reading case reports help you to determine which cases follow the same *ratio* and whether a judicial point has been made *obiter* and is therefore not the final decision on a point. A good understanding of how cases are reported – knowing the differences between judgments of a lower court and judgments on appeal; civil and criminal cases; summary judgments; case references; main judgments, concurring judgments, and dissenting judgments is fundamental. A student may find that they are reading a decision of a lower court when the judgment has been overturned on appeal. Familiarity with case law can help you identify which cases are relevant to an answer and which you can distinguish. This is also essential in oral presentations, where the assessor expects you to know and comment, on the spot, on the similarities and differences between cases.

CRITICAL REASONING AND LOGICAL ARGUMENTS

However it may be phrased, a law question expects critical reasoning from you. This is perhaps the most important element of legal work. Critical reasoning is a logical method to tackling the issues raised in a question. Very important here is your identification of alternative arguments or other possible views on an issue, and how you handle these. While you are expected to push the boundaries of the available opinion on any topic, you must do so logically and support your position with a careful review and analysis of what has already been written or said on the topic by those who are best qualified to render their opinion. This is an area the best law articles deal with very well. You will benefit greatly from reading law articles in journals and seeing how the authors examine an issue from so many different perspectives and still manage to come down on one side of the argument or the other.

Whatever your argument may be, you do have to be logical in its construction. Every statement you make in responding to a law question should lead closer to your final arguments. The importance of a logical piece of work cannot be overstated – ie that the introduction connects to the body of work and leads in a reasoned fashion to the conclusion. You cannot jump from one idea to a conclusion without clearly establishing the link between the idea and that conclusion. We can examine some legal arguments (statements with conclusions) in Table 6.1. Here I use the approach adopted in the study of philosophy, which divides an argument (statement) into two parts: premise and conclusion. In the table, each statement has been divided into its premise (first column) and the corresponding conclusion (second column). The final column will assess for critical reasoning and logic:

Table 6.1   Assessing for critical reasoning and logic

Premise	Conclusion	Critical reasoning and logic
Premise 1: All the boys in CKC are handsome. Premise 2: Amadike is a boy in CKC.	Amadike is handsome.	The parameters of this argument are fixed. The subject (Amadike) has been identified as one of a clearly defined group (the boys in CKC) all of whom share the same attribute of good looks (handsome). The critical reasoning and logic in this statement are not in doubt. The statement is appropriate.
Premise 1: Jail is a deterrent to criminal behaviour. Premise 2: David is in jail.	David will no longer commit crimes after his release from jail.	There are outstanding factors that have been overlooked in reaching the conclusion. The issue here is criminal behaviour and there are many factors that influence same, many of which are not fixed – peer pressure, greed, psychological problems, poverty etc. Should any of these factors influence David on his release, he may very well commit further crimes regardless of previous incarceration. Critical reasoning here is limited, and the statement is not logical.

Premise	Conclusion	Critical reasoning and logic
Premise 1: The FIDIC Red Book provides clauses for civil engineering contracts. Premise 2: Most practitioners prefer the FIDIC Red Book to all other standard forms of construction contracts.	The FIDIC Red Book is the best standard form of contract for civil engineering contracts.	This statement requires more evidence to support the evaluation reached in the conclusion. The premises do not reveal the benchmark for determining which standard form of construction contract is best; they do not even provide any information on the other standard forms. The opinion of "most practitioners" does not necessarily confirm the superiority of the FIDIC Red Book; it could well be that this is actually the only standard form known to those who hold this opinion. The absence of qualitative assessment of the provisions of the FIDIC Red Book in comparison with others also reveals the absence of critical reasoning here and the poor logic in this argument. The premises provided do not support the conclusion; the statement is faulty.
Premise 1: The recent banking crisis started off in the US in 2008. Premise 2: In the course of investigating banks affected, poor management and the absence of any serious obligation in corporate social responsibility were revealed. Premise 3: Companies in developing countries are poorly managed.	Banks in developing countries are not socially responsible.	Critical reasoning is lacking here. The premises do not follow each other, and there are absent considerations even in the premises themselves. For instance, although it is implied, it is not clear that the results of the investigations point to the crisis, as mentioned in Premise 1. Premise 3 has no relation with the previous two; it stands alone in its assumption. It refers to a broader subject category (companies, not banks) and does not examine, in any depth, the mentioned issue of corporate social responsibility. There is no basis for the conclusion which has only brought in a completely new factor. The statement fails for both critical reasoning and logic.

Critical reasoning and logic are ultimately about clear step-by-step thinking. Perhaps it is fair to say that this may be more obvious to a reader than the writer because, for the reader, the material is new. Although your work has examined arguments and counter-arguments, a logical piece will clearly show a unifying thread running from the start of your work to its end and establish the basis for conclusions that have been reached.

7 Critical Analysis

Tutor comments: "30%: This is not a story writing competition."
Student: "But you said to write in my own words!"

Although we have mentioned critical analysis previously, its importance demands that we elaborate a little more on this very essential aspect of a good law paper for emphasis, since it will help to gain good grades in your assessments. The following pointers will help:

ORIGINALITY

When you are asked a question, you are expected to provide a fresh insight to the question. That fresh insight will come from a thorough appreciation of the many facets in a question and a well-thought-out approach to giving a comprehensive answer.

Beware a common error which arises from heavy reliance on reported information. While an excellent research approach is always to be commended, there is a difference between writing a report on collated material and writing your own analysis on a given topic. You may think that copious reference to primary and secondary material is the indicator of a good piece of work. This is not so. If your work is mainly a reproduction of existing material, with little or no analysis of your own, there are two possible problems. The first is that there is likely to be an absence of synthesis, ie that your work is a coherent whole and that each part leads on to the other (exhibiting that single unifying thread mentioned earlier). The second is that when you rely too heavily on gathering diverse material, you will find it more difficult to focus on the specific issue you are addressing, as you will unknowingly be attempting to insert all the information you have so painstakingly gathered. You do need to be ruthless here. The test is not so much about how extensive your reading list is but that you have read what is essential to your topic or question and that you have managed to produce something cogent out of that reading list. Be ruthless – cut out the chaff. Ensure that what you submit is an original piece and not just a reproduction of all you have read or your untested opinion on an issue.

INDEPENDENT THOUGHT

Originality depends a lot on a student's capacity for independent thought. This is where students often have a problem, especially with longer pieces of work such as dissertations or take-home assignments such as coursework. There is often so much information available that the student throws in as much material as possible without any attempt to review and critically analyse the content of the literature. Guard against merely putting forward other people's opinions. A sure sign that there is little or no independent thought in a piece of work is that there are copious quotations or other people's opinions have been paraphrased or re-worded: not only is the work full of copied material, which may suggest plagiarism: there is no attempt to develop any idea from what has been read or researched.

A critical piece of work should exhibit an ability to appraise information and to deduce or induct results from that information. Without critical analysis, a piece of work loses any identifiable objective; it is almost impossible to see the purpose of the piece of work or the intent of the student who merely reproduces other people's opinion or information.

Should you need to undertake surveys or obtain samples of participants' opinion, you are still expected to engage in critical analysis of the information obtained. Thus, where you have collected data for your work, the results must be clearly presented and discussed. (Note that merely reproducing another person's data is copying and without any relevant analysis of the data to your work is of little value.) Your data must be interpreted appropriately; it is not for the assessor to interpret the results of your data collection. Tables and graphs should be accompanied by written explanations of the basis and rationale for undertaking the research in the first instance. There should be an initial review of existing data and a comparative assessment of how your data differs from that already in existence. The results obtained must also justify the data collection; there is often a mistaken belief that it is enough merely to submit data without showing how this data assists in bringing that fresh insight on the issue under analysis.

Note that your research and background reading should be as comprehensive as you can manage but, given the wealth of information now available in libraries, research centres and online resources, it is now much easier for a student not to engage in critical analysis but to reproduce the information readily available. Avoid this.

EXCESSIVE QUOTING

There is no need to quote long passages in your work except where this is unavoidable. Copious quotations give the impression that you are not very comfortable with analysing the content of the law you are citing and that you do not understand the material you have read. By all means, make reference to legal provisions, judgments, or academic publications but restrict quotations to what is absolutely necessary. Another problem with extensive quoting is that the crux of your argument may be lost. Bear in mind that you need to set out the most important and salient aspects of a legal instrument to which you are referring. Ask yourself whether a quote directly supports or clarifies your argument and the issues you are discussing. If not, leave it out.

CHECKLIST WHILE READING

When reading a piece of work for your background research, the following questions can help to make sure you are on the right track to writing up a good answer:

- Do I understand what this work is all about?
- What is the author's perspective on the issue?
- Can I distinguish my view from those of the authors in the books I read?
- Am I able to extract useful information from the material I am reading?
- Can I put useful information I have read into my own words without plagiarising?
- Are there alternatives to the arguments raised in an article or textbook?
- Have I consulted other materials, including those that may present a contrary view?
- Is there sufficient legal analysis in what I am reading? (Particularly relevant when reading from internet sites.)

CHECKLIST FOR WRITING UP YOUR WORK

- Are my arguments relevant to the question being asked?
- Have I managed to present and analyse alternative arguments or contrasting views?
- Have I merely copied the material I have read, with no input of my own? This must be avoided.
- Is there evidence of background research in my writing?
- Does my work show that I have given thought to the issues raised in the question?
- Is my work full of long quotations? Are they necessary?
- Does my work show that I am able to identify relevant issues?
- Is my work original?
- Is there evidence of critical reasoning and logic in my work?
- Have I referenced my work properly?

8 Legal Research and Referencing

Law student: "Oh dear! I can't remember where I got this from. It's a quotation from a case in an article I read."
Room mate: "Just write 'available online'."

I think it is fair to say that you cannot hope to get ahead in law if you have a deep aversion to reading. Reading is an inevitable part of any law programme and the sooner you become comfortable with that, the better. Of course, some students adapt more quickly than others – those who are used to reading literature may find it easier than others. Although modern teaching methods and technology have meant that websites and videos have crept into the lecture room as teaching aids, the fact is that information on law will often be found in the pages of books and journals.

Contemporary legal studies have something of a multi-disciplinary nature and you may find that obtaining real-life commentary or interviewing research subjects will lend more credence to an argument – something that was not common in the past when law research focused on purely analysing or making propositions on the law. However, legal research is for the most part library or desk based and must be appropriately referenced. This is because research into legal subjects is primarily an enquiry into a principle of law or an examination of how a legal principle works, and the means of arriving at a conclusion, ie the source of the foundations of the enquiry, must be evidenced. The key elements of legal research and referencing are discussed below.

LEGAL RESEARCH

Whether you are writing a short research paper such as a piece of coursework or a longer piece such as a Master's dissertation or a Ph.D. thesis, legal research will consist of a lot of reading and constructive analysis. Those primary sources of law mentioned earlier – legislation and case law – must be consulted *and read*. Excellent library staff are a bonus both for the law teacher and for the law student, as they can readily give direction and guidance on how to find and access these primary sources, and the secondary sources too. You will do well to be polite to them! Technological advancements in education have meant that it is much easier to get your hands on a journal article or a book. There are online libraries and e-books; we can access written work on our personal computers and our phones; and we can borrow material from different libraries if our local library does not have the material we want in stock. However, it also means that it is increasingly difficult to avoid doing research by pleading the absence of any available or relevant material.

There are still some difficulties, such as obtaining material only available in a different language (say, for example, that you are researching the law in a country in the Middle East which is only available in Arabic and you do not speak or read the language). It could also be, for example, that you cannot find journal articles or other material in academic published form. However, there is, as in the former, the option of official translations which may be costly but necessary. In the latter case, the challenges may lie in finding alternative verifiable materials. Such alternatives may include legislation (almost every country today has written laws which can be accessed) and reference to unreported cases where law reports are not available, or are not published, by accessing case files from court records. This will require visiting the courts to obtain this information. You may also be able to obtain information from secondary sources, including conference papers, reports, newspapers and reputable journals and magazines, company reports, business documents, government reports etc. The important thing is to be able to reference the material you consult appropriately and to be able to present the material, for instance a conference paper or newspaper article, if asked to do so. This is particularly important in jurisdictions that are still developing a tradition for academic publishing. Your research in such circumstances, challenging though it may be, is also a significant contribution to the growth of knowledge in this area and should be embraced, not shied away from.

As mentioned earlier, increasing cross-disciplinary work and study means that some empirical first-hand research may be necessary. For instance, while writing on the efficacy of a form of dispute resolution in the construction industry, for example adjudication, there may be need for input from practitioners (in the construction industry). This can be ascertained by asking some of them to fill out prepared questionnaires or perhaps by conducting interviews with those who have established practices in the field of dispute resolution in that industry. It may therefore be of use to know the means by which you can undertake such research. There are good texts on empirical research available and a good library can direct you to more extensive publications in this area. The basic points below are worth noting if you are considering further empirical research in your law essay, especially for a dissertation.

CHECKLIST FOR RESEARCH WORK

- First, identify and use the main legislation, case law and academic writing available on the topic.
- Be sure that you have covered the legal arguments sufficiently. Empirical research will be an invaluable extra but not the main part of your law research.
- Are there any ethical issues raised, for example conducting experiments with humans or animals; safety considerations; are you investigating potentially dangerous persons; do you have appropriate permits to access data or locations?
- Are you able to carry out statistical analysis? You will need this in order to evaluate any quantitative information you gather – questionnaires and sample surveys.
- Have you identified relevant and willing participants? This is essential if you intend to undertake qualitative research by interviewing persons or groups.
- Questionnaires must cover your research topic appropriately and your questions must be clear, focused, and unambiguous.
- The results of your research must fall in line with your research topic.
- Ensure that your data analysis and results are correct and verifiable and that these are clearly set out in your essay.
- You will need to provide the relevant materials used – for example, questionnaires should be attached to your essay.
- Have you assessed and complied with any requirements and ethical undertakings such as confidentiality, consent of participants to publication of research findings etc?

REFERENCING

There are some very good guides on how to cite legal material, such as the Oxford Standard for the Citation of Legal Authorities (OSCOLA). There are also several others on the different referencing methods (such as Chicago and Harvard). Institutions and academic publishers may have their preferred referencing guides. These will tell you how to cite authors' names; for instance, some will require surname first before forenames and others will prefer initials first and then the surname. They will also specify information that must be included in a citation: name, publisher, year of publication, edition, page number etc. Although footnotes as opposed to endnotes are typically used for a law paper, follow the guidelines set out in the instructions for your piece of work.

There are two points to note in referencing. The first is the common problem of "copying and pasting". A student can ask: "What if I already see what I want to say in an article or book. Can't I just copy or paraphrase it?" It is all very well to refer to existing opinion. However, you must still acknowledge the source of that opinion, whether you have copied it verbatim or paraphrased it, ie put it in your own words. The second point follows from the first. A student can also raise the query: "I have referenced every single thing I derived from another source and yet I am told that my work is not good enough." The point of academic work and the law essay in particular is that you are expected to gather information but, even more, to think independently, to analyse the information you have gathered critically and to provide a credible summation of your work. Therefore, as pointed out earlier, where your work is full of excessive quotations or is essentially a compilation of paraphrased material (which really means that you have expended a huge effort in putting other people's ideas together with little or no independent analysis of your own), the requirements for originality and objectivity are not satisfied. Without these, even the best pieces of research are not good enough if they are being judged for their *academic* merit.

CHECKLIST FOR REFERENCING

The following points can help keep you on track:

- Do not copy another person's work.
- Do not cite your class or lecture notes as legal authority.

- Do not cite lecture slides and handouts as legal authority.
- There must be a clear difference between *your* opinion and another person's.
- Use appropriate legal authority – the primary sources are your main authority for law essays.
- Cite your sources appropriately – use the citation style to which you have been referred. Do not manufacture a referencing style for yourself.
- Cite case names or other identifiers (this can be a case number) if the names of the parties are not provided in a text.
- Avoid extensive quotations.
- Do not be lazy – explain what you have read; don't just reproduce it.

9 Oral Presentations and Mooting

"The eyes eat first." (Igbo, West African proverb)

Oral presentations and mooting are increasingly being used for assessing students' work, as they can help an assessor to determine whether the student can present, in a more interactive manner, what has been learned. It is also essential practice: public speaking and good command of language are vital for a successful career not only in the law – the person who speaks well and who does so with confidence is invariably listened to!

Where oral presentation is adopted as assessment, it is important to be well prepared – good preparation will help you to be relaxed and to speak with confidence. A common form of assessment, mainly in competitions, is the moot – a popular activity in law studies and highly encouraged in the best law faculties and schools around the world. A moot competition is an excellent opportunity for any student to improve their public speaking abilities, confirm their grasp of the law and develop a whole host of talents and skills. Some students think a mooting competition is an extra activity that is not helpful (where, as is typical, the competition does not count towards the academic grades for the student). This is a misguided approach to legal education, and indeed to education in general. If you have the chance to participate in a mooting competition and you can do it – take it. You will work hard, but you will gain even more.

Whether it is for a moot, or for an assessed piece of work within a law school, at oral presentations you put forward your own conceptualisation of an issue; you think on your feet, developing an ability to respond to others on the merits of your views on a particular issue. You learn how to communicate and to do so effectively as quickly as possible because you have a limited time in which to present your argument. There is a critical difference between mooting and real-life courts – there are not usually time limits for the lawyer to make their case, save at the discretion of the court, and the lawyer does not face cross-examination!

There is great scope for character building in oral presentations. A great many friendships are made over the endless cups of coffee and long hours spent preparing for an oral assessment or competition – if you are able to reason with someone, you are more likely to have an enduring friendship with them. Oral presentations also test one's ability to remain calm under pressure; the capacity to accept correction or concede defeat; they also demand humility (which is necessary to acknowledge and correct errors) and good sportsmanship (playing fairly by the rules and sharing in your or another's success). To be honest, I have yet to meet a student who was harmed by participating in a moot or whose grades and academic performance were not positively impacted when the lessons learned from oral assessments were put into practice.

It is, of course, not just fun: an oral presentation still requires extensive background research and a good knowledge of how to apply the law and legal authority to the question. It requires good communication skills. A calm approach to presenting and rebutting arguments without coming across as a bore or argumentative will impress an assessor. There are a few further points that must be kept in view.

BE PREPARED

An assessor can tell very quickly how prepared you are for an oral presentation almost as soon as you get into your first argument. Ensure that your knowledge is up to date and that you can distinguish cases where relevant. Study your argument and know its strengths and weaknesses: know these by heart. Consider possible counter-arguments and questions that can be put to you and address these beforehand. Unless you will be reading out a script (very unlikely), write down points so that you can refer to these quickly when you are making your presentation. You can also highlight parts of your written material or use coloured identifiers to mark out pages to which you may refer for quotes etc. Make sure that you have covered as much ground as you can while doing your research, to avoid going blank when you are asked questions.

LOVE YOUR MIRROR: PRACTISE

The best public speakers are only as good as they practise. Oral presentations are a "one shot" chance to make a favourable impression (from a grade point of view, of course) and you must be fluent and organised in order to do this.

Love your mirror; practise in front of it. The mirror is especially useful for gaining a good grip on nerves and to help weed out any bad habits, such as pulling your hair, tugging your ears, or pulling at your clothes while you are speaking. It also helps to practise making eye contact – an essential tool when speaking to others. Should you be tired of this solitary admiration, practising in front of an attentive audience can also help, especially if this is an audience that understands the question, such as your colleagues. However, do not be reassured by kind words of encouragement alone; ensure that you have prepared your legal argument very well and can deliver this fluently. Again: practise!

DRESS APPROPRIATELY

If you are required to wear formal clothing, you would probably be told in advance. Generally, however, aim to dress appropriately. Keep head hair and facial hair neat. Make-up, if used, must not be garish; it should be applied neatly whether worn in bright or subdued colours. Clothes should be clean, neat and well pressed. Avoid clothes that call unnecessary attention – torn jeans, low-cut blouses and very short skirts or dresses. You should, of course, be comfortable in your clothes but be careful that you do not distract the assessors to your disadvantage.

OBSERVE THE JUDGING CRITERIA

There may be different criteria for different presentations but three things are always constant: (1) the ability to tackle issues and a good application of legal authority; (2) efficient response to questions put by the assessor; and (3) complying with the rules and instructions given.

OTHER POINTS TO NOTE

The following points are also essential:

- If there is a written component to an oral presentation or moot, make sure that you execute this equally well, as your grade for the written aspect can significantly impact your overall performance.

- Maintain eye contact with the panel or your audience.
- Speak up – enough to be heard.
- Speak clearly and pause where necessary to keep attention.
- Be respectful and courteous. Impressions really matter.
- Listen. Stop speaking when the assessor wishes to raise an issue or ask a question.
- Pay attention to the questions you are asked. Often these are a chance to elaborate on a good point; or to distinguish facts, cases or arguments; or to move on to another point.
- Avoid nervous habits. They distract you and call the assessor's attention to your discomfort instead of to your words.
- Be conscious of the allocated time. You must cover your grounds as fully as possible and so do move on to another point rather than labour one to the disadvantage of others. Finishing too quickly is also a problem; it suggests and indeed may be evidence of insufficient material.
- Think quickly. You invariably have to respond to questions you may not have thought of ahead of time.
- Do not plagiarise, even here. If you are quoting another's view, you must state this clearly. Refer directly to judges, cases, authors and their works, if you use these.
- Go over feedback given and incorporate this in future, where practicable.

Oral presentation and mooting are beneficial not just for the grades, or for the satisfaction of competing in and winning moots – they are a real chance to practise self-development.

10 Academic Conduct and Professional Ethics

Law student: "I will represent anyone. As the saying goes, 'I'm a lawyer not a moralist'."

Classmate at law clinic: "Great! I need a student representative. I was caught cheating in our exams."

Law studies do not only aim to provide you with a qualification. They should also inculcate in the law student the accepted codes of behaviour expected of a legal professional: courtesy, integrity and discipline. The law student should exhibit a high standard of courtesy towards colleagues and tutors, and approach his studies with discipline and integrity. In any event, it is not only law that expects courtesy towards others; it is inherent in higher education institutional rules that students should exhibit these values. Failure to abide by these may give rise to accusations of academic misconduct. For our purposes, academic misconduct can be divided into two broad categories: plagiarism, where sources used for work, written and oral, are not acknowledged; and the more general form of misconduct – cheating. Some institutions may categorise various forms of misconduct independently of each other and so the term can cover a broader spectrum – plagiarism, collusion, cheating, copying, bribery, coercion etc

PLAGIARISM

Plagiarism arises where an author presents work without appropriately acknowledging and referencing the sources used. This acknowledgement is a form of academic courtesy – while it is obviously a sign that you recognise that the work of others deserves credit, hence it is read in the first place, referring to that work by referencing and citing it appropriately clearly gives the credit due to the originator of the idea or opinion. It averts any suggestion that the author falsely wishes to present another's work as his own.

The following are instances of plagiarism:

- copying and pasting from the internet without referencing;
- quoting others without acknowledging the source of the quote;
- paraphrasing another's work without acknowledging the originator of the idea stated.

The most important rule of thumb to avoid plagiarism is: reference whatever is not your own original idea.

Some students may have problems with determining whether something is so commonly known that it need not be referenced. Let us consider some examples:

> "The UK comprises England and Wales, Scotland and Northern Ireland. None of these units of the country has escaped the problem of rising unemployment."

Some statements, such as this one, can be so well known that there will be no need to provide a reference – it may already be common knowledge. There is no requirement to prove the writer's knowledge or source. Contrast the statement above with the following example:

> "There is no sign of an improvement in employment figures despite various pieces of proposed legislation from the UK Parliament. The unemployment rate has remained at around 5 per cent since the start of this recession."

The first sentence is an analysis of the economic situation in the UK and the efforts made by government to address it. The second purports to buttress this analysis by providing a figure on the unemployment rate. This figure requires a clear identification of its source. The writer will therefore need to provide further information on where the figure was obtained, preferably from a direct source rather than simply citing news on the media. (There is nothing wrong with this when the originator of such information is part of the media. However, such statistical figures are usually obtained from researchers such as a statistical office, a research institution or individual or a government department. It is this direct source that should be cited.)

The two examples above feature both commonly available information and information that requires further verification. We can attempt to put these statements together in an expanded paragraph, as shown below:

"It could be considered that because the UK comprises England and Wales, Scotland and Northern Ireland, the larger market area should provide a better buffer against rising unemployment for young school leavers. However, with the UK unemployment rate remaining at an average 5 per cent since the start of the present recession in 2008, none of these units of the country has escaped what is now a troubling issue not just for the school leavers but for the entire country in general. More worrying is that there is no sign of an improvement in the employment figures in the short term despite the various pieces of employment-boosting legislation proposed by the UK Parliament."

If the above information is written in a newspaper, we do not expect that it will provide citations for the source of the information beyond the name of the journalist. If it is a serious newspaper, it will perhaps refer to the source of the statistics it has quoted. For an academic piece of work, however, more is required. We can isolate the sentences above and determine which sentence must be referenced and citation provided in order to avoid plagiarism. We do this in Table 10.1:

Table 10.1   Avoiding plagiarism

"It could be considered that because the UK comprises England and Wales, Scotland and Northern Ireland, the larger market area should provide a better buffer against rising unemployment for young school leavers." [No citation required unless this is the view of another, for example the opinion of an author in an article, book, internet piece etc.] Note that if the above is a direct quotation, it should be clearly established by the use of quotation marks adopted to distinguish word-for-word quotes.	This is an assessment of the situation in the UK and the expectation that a larger market area will mean more jobs for school leavers. It is possible that this is the writer's view. However, it is also likely that the statement is a paraphrasing of another's opinion, whether sourced from the internet or from printed matter. Note that where such a statement has been obtained from another source –whether it has been lifted directly (such as by the infamous "copy and paste" method) or paraphrased, it must be referenced appropriately since, in such an event, it is not the writer's independent view.

"However, with the UK unemployment rate remaining at an average 5 per cent since the start of the present recession in 2008" [Citation required.]	This information is clearly sourced from a statistical report. It may very well be that it is the result of the writer's empirical research, in which case information on the research itself needs to be provided. Where it has been obtained from another statistical office or report, the source must likewise be cited.
"none of these units of the country has escaped what is now a troubling issue not just for the school leavers but for the entire country in general" [Citation may be required.]	There is a mix of analysis and derived information here. The first part of the sentence "none of these units of the country has escaped ... " presents a summation of the situation across the UK. What is the basis of this summation? It could, of course, be from the same source as the 5 per cent figure in the preceding sentence or it could be from another source. Whatever information has been provided, this summation should be cited.
"More worrying is that there is no sign of an improvement in the employment figures in the short term" [Citation may be required.] Note that if the above is a direct quotation, it should be clearly established by the use of quotation marks adopted to distinguish word-for-word quotes.	This part of the last sentence is another summation of the UK employment situation in light of the 2008 recession. Just as for the first sentence in the paragraph, it could be an independent assessment by the writer, in which case it does not require referencing. However, if this statement is borne out of the information found in the course of researching the topic and has been paraphrased or lifted directly, it is only appropriate to cite the source clearly.

| "despite the various pieces of employment-boosting legislation proposed by the UK Parliament" [Citation may be required.] | This last bit could very well be a continuation of the preceding words as immediately above. However, I have deliberately broken it up because of the implied information here, ie that there is proposed legislation that will address the rising unemployment. Which legislation is referred to here? It is not sufficient to suggest information without more detail, where such information is material to the topic and can throw more light on your analysis. Unless the various pieces of proposed legislation are going to be mentioned in the paragraph itself, the statement is better served by citing the proposed legislation in the footnotes. |

CHEATING

"Cheating" is used here as a general term covering impersonation or getting others to impersonate a student at an exam; taking prohibited material into examinations; copying another person's work; providing false information in your own work, such as creating fictitious cases; and getting others to do your work, including bribing them to sit your exams or tests or to do your coursework. Sometimes students cannot understand why they are penalised for working together. Where unauthorised, this is deemed to be collusion and, while it may not be called cheating *per se*, it is still academic misconduct. On many occasions, two or more students work together, sometimes innocently, on an assessment or project that requires independent work. However, unless you have been assigned a team or asked to work in groups, every piece of assessed work must be undertaken independently.

The point is that your work should be a product of your own genuine effort. Educational institutions each have their approach to tackling academic misconduct and you will no doubt be informed of this. It is fundamental that you steer clear of becoming embroiled in such matters. Many professional careers have suffered for later speculations and, at times, proof that an individual was guilty of academic misconduct during their studies.

PROFESSIONAL ETHICS

Law is a professional discipline with its own ethics and accepted codes of behaviour. In the course of legal "professional" training, those values mentioned earlier – courtesy, integrity and discipline – form part of the ethics in the standard practice course for prospective qualified solicitors and advocates. It is only to be expected that society will demand a higher standard of decency from those who purport to work within the boundaries of the law and social norms. A lawyer may be forgiven (but certainly not forgotten, I can assure you) for having the worst dress sense but will be neither forgiven nor forgotten (and certainly not by the public) for being rude or obnoxious or for being a cheat or a fraudster.

It is preferable that you live up to the expectations that society has of you if you are going to hold yourself out as being a law professional. That includes not only dressing appropriately, especially for formal events, but even ensuring that your words, manners and letters (and that includes e-mails) are constructed properly and without causing distress or anger to the recipient. Whichever career you end up following, you will find that you will go much further when you address colleagues, clients, court officials, the court itself, and those you meet along the way, with civility. This also applies to the student: being rude in the class or discourteous in your communications, written or oral, will not endear you to anyone, least of all to the person supposed to assess your performance. Learn and inculcate the discipline of courtesy towards others. It will gradually become a habit and you will do well to adopt it.

Exam Tips

- Legibility is crucial in exams where the answers are to be handwritten. Make sure that your handwriting is legible and neat and that you have an extra pen available before you begin.

- Keep calm.

- Read the instructions carefully.

- Note the time allotted for the paper and work out for yourself how long you can reasonably spend on each question.

- Before you start writing, look through all questions and, where there are options, decide which ones you can answer best.

- Make a quick map/answer plan, noting relevant cases or legislation that come to your mind. You can do this on the first page of your answer sheet or at the back, for quick reference.

- Answer essay questions fully, using paragraphs and full sentences. A sketchy answer will do you no favours.

- Highlight cases or legislation by underlining them or using highlighters. (It is important, however, to ensure that you have emphasised the appropriate reference – you don't want to draw attention to a wrong piece of legislation!)

- Do not be in a hurry to submit your work. Take the time to read it through carefully before you hand in your paper.

- Language is important. Even in exams, your work should still be written in proper language, using appropriate legal terminology.

Appendices

Note: The following are only outline answers. A student faced with these questions, while being expected to answer along the lines of the contents of the model answers given, can also expand upon the points shown below. Note also that references for law papers are typically footnotes but footnotes (and case citations) will probably not be expected under exam conditions.

Appendix 1: Essay Question (International Law)

QUESTION

Analyse the following statement:

> "While they are both sources of international law, a treaty may prevail over a rule of customary international law but not if the rule of customary international law is *jus cogens*."

ANSWER

According to Art 38 of the ICJ Statute, the sources of international law include treaties, customs, general principles of law and also judicial decisions and the teachings of highly qualified public lawyers, in this order. The hierarchy of sources is not expressly stated but is rather implied from the arrangement of these sources in the provision. In this paper, treaties will first be defined and then a distinction made between those and rules of customary international law. The primacy of *jus cogens* over both categories of sources of international law will then be examined.

Treaties may be referred to in a variety of ways, including "conventions", "charters" and "agreements". They may be bilateral or multipartite. They are written agreements between states and accepted as binding between them. They establish the relations between them in respect of the subject of the treaty and set out clear provisions on how the treaty applies to the parties *inter se*. They are governed by international law. On the other hand, a rule of customary international law is not necessarily written (although a treaty provision may incorporate a rule of customary international law, as the ICJ noted in *Libya* v *Chad* in respect of Art 31 of the Vienna Convention on the Law of Treaties).

A rule of customary international law is one derived from the constant and uniform practice of states in respect of the subject-matter of the rule, such practice accompanied by *opinio juris sive necessitatis*: the belief by states that the practice is legally obliged of them (*Asylum* case; *North Sea Continental Shelf* cases; the *Nicaragua* case). For a state not to be bound by such a general rule, that state would have to have expressed its dissent in good time, before the rule becomes established (*Anglo-Norwegian Fisheries* case).

Where there is no conflict between a treaty provision and a rule of customary international law, that is where both a treaty and a rule of customary law are identical or similar, the application of either source will not negate the status of the other. Indeed, one buttresses the other and each will be considered on its own merits. This was the view of the ICJ in the *Nicaragua* case. In that case, the ICJ was of the view that while it had to consider the application of Arts 2(4) and 51 of the UN Charter to US military actions in Nicaragua and whether these actions had violated the provisions on the use of force, the court was not precluded from considering the customary international law rules on the use of force.

However, where a rule of customary international law comes into conflict with a treaty provision, the provisions of the treaty may, *prima facie*, supersede the rule of customary international law. In the *Wimbledon case*, the PCIJ had to consider the effect of Art 380 of the Treaty of Versailles. In that case, Germany had refused to allow the passage of an English Steamship, the *SS Wimbledon*, carrying military materials to Poland, via the Kiel Canal. Germany had argued that, under customary international law, the relevant rule in this case was that no passage was allowed through the territory of a neutral state to the territory of a belligerent state. Germany argued that it was a neutral state and was thus within its rights to refuse entry to the steamship.

The applicants (Poland, together with Britain, France, Italy and Japan), argued that Art 380 of the Treaty of Versailles provided for the free passage of vessels of commerce and of war belonging to countries which were not at war with Germany. As the *SS Wimbledon* belonged to a country not at war with Germany, it was therefore entitled to free passage through the Kiel Canal. The PCIJ, noting that the Treaty was an international agreement entered into by Germany and the Allied powers, was of the view that the provision of the Treaty prevailed over any previous rules to the contrary. The PCIJ therefore held that since Germany had been a party to the

Treaty, it was bound by the provisions of the Treaty and was wrong to disallow the free passage of a ship belonging to a country with which it was not at war.

In spite of this decision, treaties are usually constructed and construed as agreements based on customary law rules. They are therefore not expected to alter or derogate from the latter unless the parties to the Treaty expressly agree this to be their intention. The caveat to this is that treaties which conflict with peremptory norms of general international law will be void. These peremptory norms referred to as *jus cogens* are those rules which have been accepted and recognised by the international community as a whole as having peremptory force and which cannot be derogated from (Art 53 Vienna Convention on the Law of Treaties). In the aforementioned *Nicaragua* case, the ICJ stated that the prohibition against the use of force was *jus cogens* since this was recognised and accepted by the international community. Again, in the case of *Siderman de Blake* v *Republic of Argentina*, the court held that freedom from official torture is a norm of *jus cogens*: "a right deserving of the highest status under international law". Furthermore, by virtue of Art 64 of the Vienna Convention, a new peremptory norm accepted as *jus cogens* will prevail over an existing treaty provision with which it is in conflict.

International law therefore recognises the supremacy of certain rules of customary international law as norms which cannot be derogated from even under a written international agreement such as a treaty. These norms include prohibitions on genocide, torture, slavery, the use of force and the right to self-determination and they will prevail over an existing or future provision in a treaty. As international law continues to evolve, it may well be that there will be other rules of customary international law not presently recognised as such, but which in future may attain the status of peremptory norms of general international law and which will therefore also come to prevail over existing or subsequent conflicting treaty provisions. In view of the considerations above, a treaty may supersede a rule of customary international law but not if the latter is *jus cogens*.

Appendix 2a: Problem Question (Company Law)

Jinxed & Jammed Ltd is a private company which has been trading for 6 years. One of its two directors (the directors are the only members) is concerned that the company has been unable to pay its debts to some creditors because of insufficient funds. The other director asserts that the company can still be rescued as a going concern. Advise them on what to do to ensure this. Will your answer be different if:

(a) The holder of a floating charge or the court appoints an administrator?
(b) The company is in Scotland and Janet, a business woman based there, has a floating charge over the property of the company?

ANSWER

The main issues that arise in this problem centre on insolvency and liquidation, or winding up, of companies. Insolvency is a situation where the company is no longer able to make good its debts to creditors and there is a chance that it may be able to carry on trading. Liquidation refers to a process where a company which is no longer able to trade is dissolved or wound up. It may arise as a result of insolvency, although it is also possible that a company's constitution may have provided for its dissolution after a specified period.

Insolvency procedures include administrative receivership, administration, and voluntary arrangements. Liquidation procedures are members' voluntary winding-up (for solvent companies), creditors' voluntary winding-up (for insolvent companies), and winding-up by the court. Given the company's directors' interests in rescuing the company as a going concern, the applicable procedure will be administration, under insolvency. The applicable rules will be the provisions of the Insolvency Act 1986 (IA 1986).

For administration, an administrator (A) has to be appointed. A is an officer of the court appointed by the court, the holder of a floating charge, a company or a company's director (ss 7 and 8 of and Sch B1 to IA 1986). The appointment to be made here should be in line with Sch B1, para 22 to the Act. The purposes of administration are: to rescue the company as a going concern; or to achieve better results for creditors than by liquidation; to realise property in order to make a distribution to one or more secured or preferential creditors. It is important therefore that an administrator who is a qualified insolvency practitioner as provided for under ss 388–391A of IA 1986 is appointed to ensure that these objectives are achieved.

The appointment of an administrator must also be notified to a court with jurisdiction. No appointment can be made if another insolvency procedure (apart from voluntary arrangement) is going on or is being considered. The director must bear in mind that administration expenses have priority in the settlement of the company's debts.

With regard to whether this answer would be different if the holder of a floating charge or the court appoints an administrator, the Act specifies that where, prior to the filing of the notice of an appointment, an appointment is made by a court or by the holder of a floating charge, this appointment supersedes the appointment by a director: Sch B1, para 33 to IA 1986. If the company is in Scotland and Janet, who is based there, has a floating charge over the property of the company, s 122(2) of IA 1986 will apply. Under those provisions, in Scotland, a company which the Court of Session has jurisdiction to wind up may be wound up by the court if there is subsisting a floating charge over property comprised in the company's property and undertaking, and the court is satisfied that the security of the creditor entitled to the benefit of the floating charge is in jeopardy.

A creditor's security is in jeopardy if the court is satisfied that events have occurred or are about to occur which mean that leaving the company to retain power to dispose of the property which is subject to the floating charge may not be in the creditor's interest. As the holder of a floating charge, Janet may therefore apply to the court to appoint an administrator and if she does this before the director files an application for an administrator, her application will have precedence over the latter. If, on the other hand, she applies to the court for a winding-up (as distinct from administration), the court in Scotland may also consider the merits of her case.

Appendix 2b: Problem Question (Business Law)

Note: This question is reproduced by kind permission of my teaching colleagues at Robert Gordon University.

QUESTION

George, Brad and Julia each put some money into a restaurant venture. There is no written agreement, but they did agree that the venture would last for 3 years and that it couldn't be brought to an end before this just by one of them giving notice. They also agreed orally that purchases for anything other than routine food and drink supplies had to be agreed in advance by all three. When they started out, George, the chef, said he wasn't interested in taking part in managing the firm and thought that if things didn't work then the other two should bear any losses or liabilities incurred. The firm has been in business now for 4 years without any change to its terms and conditions of operation.

Brad took it upon himself to order new furniture for the restaurant and to review the wine list, buying in some much more expensive wines than before without consulting George or Julia. George ignored the sell-by date on and unpleasant smell from some chicken fillets and used them up in a curry. As a result, 10 customers went down with salmonella poisoning. Brad got angry with George, they got into a fight and now George has a broken nose and his Armani glasses are damaged beyond repair.

Julia is fed up with both of them. She wants to get out of the partnership to set up in business with her boyfriend Andy.

ANSWER

The legal issues from the scenario above arise with respect to partnerships. They include: the formation and existence of a partnership; the conditions for termination and dissolution of a partnership; the relationship and duty of partners towards each other; the liability of a firm and of partners; the duty of partners to third parties; and the liability of a partner for debts and obligations after the dissolution of a partnership. The applicable rules are the rules on partnership as provided for under the 1890 Partnership Act.

In this scenario, George, Brad and Julia have entered into an agreement to run a restaurant, initially for 3 years, with a view to making profit. They intend to enter into a business for a limited purpose and duration (*Mair v Wood*) which is a joint venture, and which is a kind of partnership. Their agreements on how to run the restaurant have been made orally and there is no written agreement between them. However, a partnership under the 1890 Act can be made orally, in writing or inferred from the conduct of the parties. It therefore suffices that they are in agreement, that they have made this agreement orally and that they set up the restaurant with a view to make a profit. A partnership can be said to exist on this basis between the three as it can be inferred from their conduct and their oral agreement: s 1 of the Partnership Act 1890; *Dollar Land v CIN Properties*.

The venture should have expired after 3 years but they have continued, so it will be taken that they have continued with their original intentions (s 27(1) and (2)) as a partnership at will (s 26(1)).

Although they could agree orally over their terms, ie no need for a written agreement, George cannot limit his liabilities as a partner since partners are liable jointly and severally in Scotland (s 9). He cannot contract out of these as well with respect to debts to third parties (ss 10 and 12).

The Partnership Act 1890 provides that partners should act in utmost good faith towards each other (s 28). This was reiterated in the case of *Ferguson v Mackay*. Therefore Brad owed a duty to his partners to inform them of his improvisations, particularly with regard to the acquisition of furniture which is clearly contrary to the terms of their agreement. With regard to the purchase of expensive wines, however, should Brad have incurred any liabilities on this, Julia and George may not be bound by his actions if the third parties ought to have known that he was acting beyond his authority (s 8 of the 1890 Act; *Paterson v Gladstone Bros*) which may be the case as they should have been on alert when he made requests for non-routine supplies. Excepting this, Julia and George, who are with him in the partnership, are bound by Brad's actions owing to the nature of partnership liability under the Partnership Act (s 12).

A firm's liability is limited to acts done to third parties (ss 10 and 11). As such, George cannot hold the firm liable for injury to his glasses or his nose. He may, however, sue Brad privately if he wishes. Liability for the food poisoning will be on all the parties towards the customers who suffered food poisoning – jointly and severally if it occurred in Scotland (ss 9, 10 and 12; *Mair v Wood*).

Under s 32 of the Act, Julia ought to be able to give notice at any time to George and Brad since they have continued as a partnership at will (s 26), given that the original fixed term has expired (s 27(2)). However, at the start, they did agree orally that the venture could not be brought to an end just by one of them giving notice. Therefore, Julia may then apply to the court for dissolution of the partnership. She can do so on the ground of prejudicial conduct under s 35C since Brad and George have got into a fight; Brad is acting beyond his powers by ordering expensive wines and furniture; and George, who is the chef, is not taking care of the hygiene issues in food preparation which is critical to the business. All of these are prejudicial to the profit capacity of their venture. She can also apply to the court on the ground that the others have persistently breached the agreements between them by their conduct under s35D, given that Brad has not kept the others informed of his non-routine purchases and George's actions. She can also apply for dissolution under the sweeping provisions of s 35F – that it is now just and equitable to dissolve the partnership in light of the above circumstances.

With regard to the extent of Julia's liability for debts and obligations while she was a partner, the Act provides under s 17(2) that outgoing partners are still liable for debts and obligations incurred while the partner was in the firm. However, the Act and case law provide that a retiring partner may, under an agreement with the partners and with their creditors, be discharged from these liabilities (s 17(3); *Welsh v Knarston*). In the absence of any agreement limiting her liabilities, Julia is therefore liable for all debts incurred by the firm while she was a partner.